DELTA BABY & TWO SEA SONGS

with illustrations by LYDIA DABCOVICH,
CHARLES MIKOLAYCAK & JIM ARNOSKY

Richard Kennedy

Delta Baby
& 2 sea songs

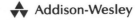 Addison-Wesley

BOOKS BY RICHARD KENNEDY

The Parrot and the Thief
The Contests at Cowlick
The Porcelain Man
The Blue Stone
Come Again in the Spring
Oliver Hyde's Dishcloth Concert
The Dark Princess
The Rise and Fall of Ben Gizzard
Delta Baby and Two Sea Songs

Text Copyright © 1979 by Richard Kennedy
Illustrations for Delta Baby Copyright © 1979 by Charles Mikolaycak
Illustrations for Stinky Pete Copyright © 1979 by Lydia Dabcovich
Illustrations for The Wreck of the Linda Dear Copyright © 1979 by James Arnosky
All Rights Reserved
Addison-Wesley Publishing Company, Inc.
Reading, Massachusetts 01867
Printed in the United States of America
ABCDEFGHIJK-WZ-79

Book designed by Charles Mikolaycak

Library of Congress Cataloging in Publication Data

Kennedy, Richard.
Delta baby & two sea songs.

CONTENTS: Delta baby. — Stinky Pete. — The wreck of
the Linda Dear.
1. Narrative poetry, American. [1. Narrative
poetry. 2. American poetry] I. Dabcovich, Lydia.
II. Mikolaycak, Charles. III. Arnosky, Jim.
IV. Title.
PZ8.3.K3835De   811'.5'4   78-6895
ISBN 0-201-03598-7

For Dennis and Tina and Abram

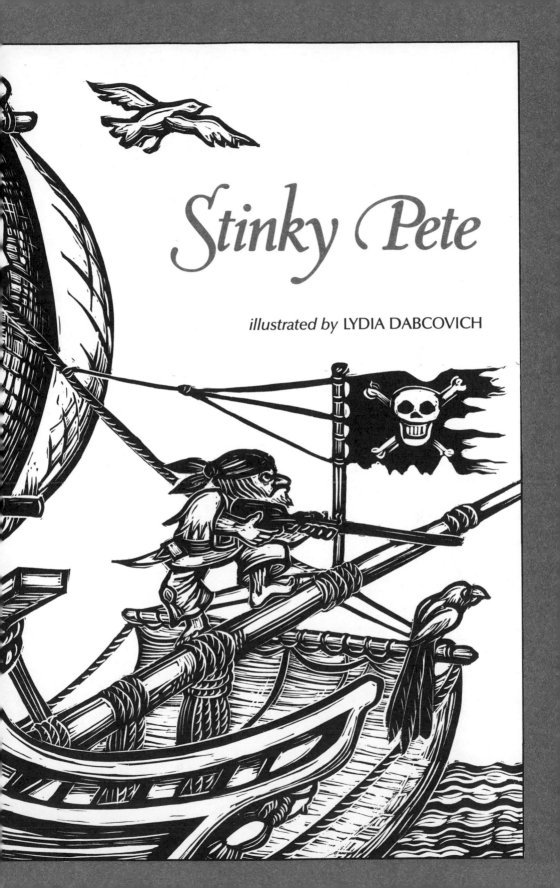

Stinky Pete

illustrated by LYDIA DABCOVICH

There sailed a pirate called Stinky Pete,
a black-hearted villian with dirty feet,
whose crew was scum from head to toe.
His first mate's name was Snotty-nose Joe.

They cut a path on the open sea,
sliced out gizzards and heard no plea
for mercy, fairness, or "In God's name!"
And dogfights next to them were tame.

So one brisk morning while out for spoil,
they spied a ship rigged up all royal,
and fancy dandies strolled the deck,
with lacey collars around their necks.

"Avast!" cried Pete, "The Lord bless me,
them fops is all dressed out for tea.
Stick 'em through their button holes,
I wouldn't cut up such fine clothes."

The scurvy crew came round to port,
slobbering curses and came athwart
the goodly ship and swung aboard,
their cruddy teeth clamped on their swords.

The men they fought were clean and shaven,
with courage to fight and not one craven,
but at close quarters they gave up trying.
The pirate's smell was worse than dying.

They all then soon gave up the fray,
dropped their swords and started to pray,
and holding their noses they all withdrew,
to the upwind side of the pirate crew.

"Run out the plank!" yelled Stinky Pete,
"The sharks are waiting for their treat."
And Snotty-nose Joe got the men all tied,
for their last short walk on over the side.

He ran his nose down his sleeve and said,
"All set, captain," and he tore a shred
of cloth from his shirt and covered the eyes
of the first of the men that was doomed to die.

He was lifted up and set on the plank,
while cutlasses poked him about the flanks,
and the scummy pirates laughed at the fun.
Stinky Pete chuckled and scratched at his bum.

Then just as the man teetered on the verge,
from out of the cabin a girl emerged.
"You there!" she cried, "You rank rapscallion!
Are you the captain of that filthy galleon?"

It was Princess Ann, out sailing for pleasure,
and she marched up to Pete and took his measure.
Said she to Pete, "You smell like a reef,
and don't you ever brush your teeth?"

"Belay that!" roared Pete, "Or I'll haul your keel!"
But she grabbed his nose and made him kneel,
and called to her Ladies who were waiting aside,
for some soap and water to scrub Pete's hide.

They got out tubs, and soaps and lotions,
and dunked the pirates in the ocean,
and scoured them all till they turned bright pink,
then sent them to wash their clothes in a sink.

"Just powder yourselves while you're there," said Ann,
They meekly turned and said, "Yes ma'am."
"Tend your nails and trim your beards,
brush your teeth and clean out your ears."

Snotty-nose Joe she took by the hair,
and from a petticoat had him tear
ten squares of cloth. "Now use a hanky
to blow your nose!" And Joe said, "Thank 'ee."

She lined them up in an hour or so,
at the poop deck rail and made them show
their ears and nails, and then she charged,
"Get over and clean up your filthy barge."

Two days working those pirates ran,
under the eye of Princess Ann.
They mopped and brushed and shined their ship,
then Ann inspected, and found it fit.

"Farewell," she called, as they drifted apart,
"You're clean outside, now clean your hearts.
If ever again you pirate this sea,
I'll catch you sure, and you'll answer to me."

So off they sailed, and Snotty-nose Joe
is now called Sniffles, and always blows.
Stinky is now called Soapy Pete,
smells of lavender, and has clean feet.

And ever since their run-in with Ann,
they've not been pirates with bloody hands,
but they trade in silks, and spices and tea,
and they're nice and sweet as sailors *can* be.

Delta Baby

illustrated by CHARLES MIKOLAYCAK

Delta baby, cry and scream,
lay upon your boat and dream.

Rocking bow and rolling beam,
sunlit morning waters stream,
grasses sparkle, fishes leap,
floating free the child sleeps.

In the moondark night before,
blood runs warm beneath his door,
torches blaze and men are slain,
the search for baby is in vain.

Near his door his mother lies,
sword in hand his father dies.

Baby is by all forsaken
but for one, and he is taken
from his crib and through the halls.
A window opens, and he falls.

Towers topple, men are crushed,
baby falls into a bush.
Smoke and fire swirl about.
"Find the baby!" someone shouts.

"Kill the baby!" others cry,
and the bush where baby lies
begins to burn, and from the flame
at awful cost the child is claimed.

He is lifted from his nest,
by a man in checkered dress,
a bloody man with hair afire,
wearing bells the child admires.

Amongst the trees and deep amid
the river's rushes he is hid.
Swords are sharpened, clubs are blunted,
everywhere the child is hunted.

In the dark he hears the tale,
of the knowing nightingale:
"Life to all and death to each,
midnight seed and daylight peach."

Birds of foam and birds of fire,
birds of barn and birds of spire,
birds of lute and birds of lyre,
sing from joy and from desire.

Set upon the sea to sail,
baby cannot tell a tale,
of his mother there's no clue,
father is a mystery, too.

Secret in a secret rolled,
mystery tucked in mystery's fold,
all there is that can be told,
baby's blanket's spun from gold.

Kingdoms rise and kingdoms fall,
"Kill the baby!" comes the call.
On the boat is writ a name
none can read, so none can blame.

Near the delta in a pool,
on his face there lays a fool,
black with blood and burned by embers,
dressed in bells the child remembers.

What has happened, what is hinted,
what is pictured, what is printed?
On the waves the boat is flowing,
perhaps a ghost is in there rowing.

Ancient lands and silent stones,
diamonds in a golden throne,
moaning winds sweep dead king's bones,
everything that's known is known.

Heaven's winds and rain will clean you,
evening birds and bugs will sing you
lullabyes, and night will bring you
sparkling beasts who will redeem you.

Delta baby cry and scream,
lay upon your boat and dream.

THE WRECK OF THE
Linda Dear

illustrated by JIM ARNOSKY

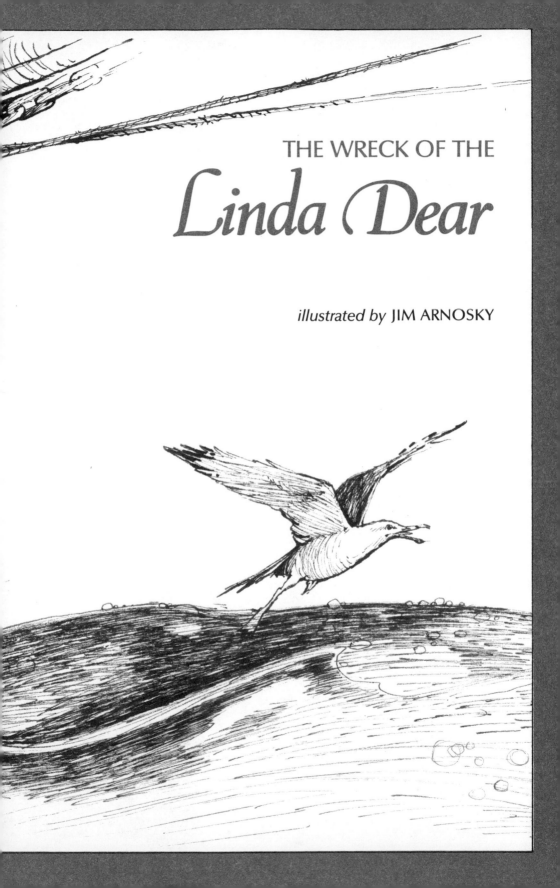

Down by the sea where I stroll sometime,
musing on poetry and making up rhyme,
I stopped for a while with a faraway look,
like a poet's picture on the back of his book.

And an old man took me by the sleeve,
and said to me, "Can you conceive
of rat as large as a sailing ship?"
"No," says I, and he patted his hip
and says, "Sit down and I'll tell you the tale
of the Linda Dear and Pacific Bill."

So down I sets myself while he
pulls at his pipe and looks at the sea,
and remembering deeply upon the past,
he stroked his beard and said at last,
"The brass was bright and the paint was new,
and we sailed with a cargo of Mulligan stew."

Well, I had better things to do
than listen to lies about a ship filled with stew,
so I said, "Excuse me, please" and got up on a knee,
"But didn't I just hear a bell strike three?"

"Sit down," says he, "and hear me now,
or I'll kick your stern end over your bow!
I've sailed these oceans for forty years,
and I've got some stories not many hears."

So again I sets and he takes my arm,
and begins once more to spin his yarn.

"All rats you know are fond of sailing,
they eat the stores and run the railings,
and we fling 'em off when we can, of course,
and watch 'em drown with no remorse.

"But the Linda Dear, I tell you, son,
had a thousand rats or it didn't have none,
and they ate up all the Mulligan stew,
and when the last of that was through,
a rat by the name of Pacific Bill
declared he hadn't ate his fill.

"So he ate a friend, and then a cousin,
his grandma next, and half a dozen
other relatives—large and small,
then rats he hardly knew at all,
and they sank in his belly in the Mulligan stew,
and his belly grew, and he did, too.

"And thirty rats later old Bill had grown
as big as a hound, and the rat's shrieks and moans
were awful to hear, but they were all through
when they slid down his gullet and splashed in the stew.
Some tried to float on the cabbage leaves,
but they sank, too, in potatoes and peas.

"Then rats came scuttling up the ladders,
and we knocked 'em off as they tried to scatter,
and rats were flying everywhere,
through the rigging and in our hair,
and the mate cried out, "Look down below!"
and me it was that had to go.

"Oh, never in your life or death
was such a sight to take your breath—
a rat as large as the galley table,
gobbling fast as he was able,
other rats, and he made a catch
to grab my boot, but I slammed the hatch.

"A rat, a rat!" to the mate I cries.
"I know they're rats, I've got good eyes!"
"No, no," I yells, "this one's a giant!"
"Amusing," says he, "but not good science."
And at that moment the deck busts through,
and Pacific Bill snatched up one of the crew."

The old man then let his head droop down,
remembering this with a tear and a frown.
He looked at me with his eyes all glistening,
"You'll let me know if you're bored with listening?"
"It's fairly interesting," I shrugged and said,
and so he continued, shaking his head.

"Well, Pacific Bill climbed up out of the hold,
and we jumped and ran and climbed and rolled.
He caught the mate and he took a bite,
and I'd never seen that man so excited.
Oh, it's awful to see a rat eat a human,
especially one of your own fellow crewmen.
And Bill chased us all around the ship,
up on the yardarms and out on the sprits.

"One by one he ate up the crew,
and the captain cried "Mutiny!" but got ate too,
till I alone, most dead with fear,
was clutching the figurehead of the Linda Dear.
I watched Pacific Bill aghast
as he ate the sails, and then a mast.

"He ate the railings, then the deck,
the wheel-house next and made a wreck
from stem to stern of our good ship,
and my grip on Linda was starting to slip.
Then that monster rat spied me,
and reached out a claw, and I dropped in the sea.

"I fell astern the ship and floated,
watching as that rat grew bloated,
eating everything in sight,
until at last with one great bite,
the ship was gone, and Pacific Bill,
he sank too, and all was still.

Now I hadn't a raft and I hadn't a dory,
but yet I'm here to tell this story.
Do you want to know," said the man with a wink,
"How I stayed afloat and didn't sink?"
"I wouldn't mind," I said with a yawn,
"If you're in the mood you might go on."

"Well, there I was, doomed to drown,
but just before the third time down,
the figurehead of the Linda Dear
popped up beside me, and I'm here
to tell this tale—none truer or straighter,
for hugging that girl till six days later
a sloop named the Bumblebat threw us a line,
hauled us aboard, and sailed us home fine."

The old man then lit his pipe with care,
gazed out to sea and said, "It's rare
the way them rats liked Mulligan stew,
and how old Bill just grew and grew,
and I reckon no man living or dead—
but me—ever loved a figurehead.

"So we got married—it was only right,
after hugging Dear Linda six days and nights.
Made a fine wife and mother, in my opinion,
had two lovely girls, and a wooden Indian."

"I'll go now," I said, "if that's the end."
"Aye," says he, "but come back again,
and I'll tell you how ninety-two pigs got free
in a howling typhoon in the China sea."

"Love to hear it," I said, "you bet."
But I've never strolled back that way yet.

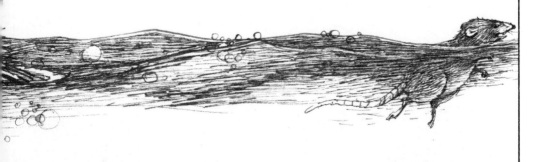

ABOUT THE AUTHOR

Richard Kennedy lives in Newport, Oregon, on the coast. He has two teen-age sons. He is living proof that confusion, fear, and scattered sensibilities need not be useless. His little house is tidy, however. Richard has written several children's books, all of which are awesome and wonderful.

ABOUT THE ARTISTS

Jim Arnosky, who lives on a farm in Vermont, has illustrated several books for children. He is the creator of *Nathaniel,* a character he claims has come to look more and more like him over the years and the hero of his most recent book for Addison-Wesley.

Lydia Dabcovich illustrated her first children's book in Israel where she grew up. She works in several media, but primarily in linoleum cuts and woodcuts. Her most recent children's picture book is *There Once Was A Woman Who Married A Man* for Addison-Wesley.

Charles Mikolaycak is both a book designer and an illustrator. His work has been consistently honored by the American Institute of Graphic Arts. He has illustrated many children's books, including *Three Wanderers From Wapping* and one selection in *Six Impossible Things Before Breakfast,* both for Addison-Wesley.